T0032027

Grappling Hook

Grappling

Hook

Sarah
Yi-Mei Tsiang

Copyright © Sarah Yi-Mei Tsiang 2022
All rights reserved

Palimpsest Press
1171 Eastlawn Ave.
Windsor, Ontario. N8S 3J1
www.palimpsestpress.ca

Printed and bound in Canada
Cover design and book typography by Ellie Hastings
Edited by Jim Johnstone

Palimpsest Press would like to thank the Canada Council for the Arts
and the Ontario Arts Council for their support of our publishing
program. We also acknowledge the assistance of the Government of
Ontario through the Ontario Book Publishing Tax Credit.

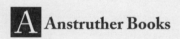 **Anstruther Books**

 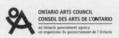 

LIBRARY AND ARCHIVES CANADA CATALOGUING IN PUBLICATION

TITLE: Grappling hook / Sarah Yi-Mei Tsiang.
NAMES: Tsiang, Sarah, 1978- author.
DESCRIPTION: Poems.
IDENTIFIERS: Canadiana (print) 20220142475
             Canadiana (ebook) 20220142505

ISBN 9781990293030 (SOFTCOVER)
ISBN 9781990293047 (EPUB)
ISBN 9781990293054 (PDF)
CLASSIFICATION: LCC PS8639.S583 G73 2022 | DDC C811/.6—DC23

Contents

For the Villanelles,
you have all inserted so much brilliance into my life!

Two Truths and a Lie

I died last year. No one has noticed yet. The bread still rises on the counter, my signature haunts permission forms. I still do the thousands of things needed to run a household. I weave my daughter's hair with fingers of wind and she leaves each day with the faint sense that we spoke, the words a half-remembered scent, like trying to conjure lilacs in August. My son climbs every tree in the backyard, taking their arms for mine, thinking that he can be cradled aloft in a bough and it will not break. My face a cloud gently tearing itself apart.

I once took a job as a minor God. Children were born in the hollows of my footprints, curled like caterpillars. I had to walk for miles, thousands of babies springing up in forests, and bogs, and along the gravel path where they spit stones with their first cries. But I was only paid to walk forwards, so Time was hired to follow me like a handmaiden, gathering children, wiping their mouths with her tongue-wet thumb, singing lullabies of erasure. Even after I quit, Time became my dogged assistant, trailing me everywhere, taking pay from my stride.

I've become a black hole. Right now, I am thinking of how I want to take you in my mouth. I promise you that my hunger is complete, so sweet, you will think you're eating instead of being eaten. I want to swallow you whole, but I will also swallow the gingerbread house, and the forest, and the stones and the river, and the sun. We can live inside my hunger, and never want for anything.

You can't see me, it's dark

Every night my husband turns to me in bed and says
　　you're beautiful
　　　　and I tell him, *you can't see me, it's dark.*
　　　　I remember what you look like he says,
and he believes this,

even as the dark sloughs off my face
and my limbs plump like a dying jellyfish
when the tides reach up, and I'm being inhaled
back into the undertow. I'm boneless

and poisonous and he says *I remember*
and only the dark, empty room
believes him.

Angstrom

I drag over the floor of the world like a grappling hook.
Everything I have no need of catches on it.
Tired indignation, glowing resignation.
The executioners gather stones, God writes in the sand.
  — Tomas Tranströmer

On night's shore, my husband crouches, one hand
dipped into the starry water. It is so cold.
Light speed is slower than extinction — we see the bodies
of stars, drink their last on summer nights.
When my husband speaks it is the same; breath
that travelled too far to feel the truth of it. Like a book
you read, weeping on the train, and no one can know you
by your tears or the words scattered on the page.
What to do with another's suffering? Look,
I drag over the floor of the world like a grappling hook

and pick up the detritus of your sadness. Small handfuls
that used to be mountains. Did you know that drowning victims
slip into the water the way you'd slip out of parties? An Irish goodbye,
no fuss, no one noticing that you had your coat on before dessert.
I remember once, handing you the baby from the dock.
You reached out and took him, then gently sank into the sunlit
lake, our son held above your watery hair. I had forgotten you
were a poor swimmer. I was angry, and laughing, and what did I have
to save you? A child's fishing rod with a blunt hook. A tackle kit.
Everything I have no need of catches on it

and I bring up waterlogged boots, seaweed, watch you disappear
into a summer
lake while the children do backflips off the dock. But this isn't the
whole truth.
You do come up for air. You roast marshmallows and catch
fireflies for our daughter. We release them in the morning,
soft as catkins from a willow, falling into their freedom.
Your face too, watching our daughter release each one, the tender
fascination
she holds for the small and vulnerable. Remember the spring
you drove me to a field of lilacs just so we could kiss among the
blossoms?
How can I be so happy when you are so sad? My joy becomes a
kind of accusation,
tired indignation, glowing resignation.

I forget sometimes, that you can be alone in a marriage
and still in love. I keep wanting to go back to the start: stars,
atoms, water.
Physics tell us what poetry only gestures to: electrons can never touch.
Here we are, hovering above our chairs, forever a distance of one
angstrom
from everything, each other. We are particle and wave, a duality
of impossible behaviors. You sit beside me, in despair, and
I reach for your hand while our minds tell us the story of our touch.
Flowers fall under the weight of the wind, I trace your lips
with my eyes closed. We are travelling to the same land;
the executioner gathers stones, god writes in the sand.

12

i.

At night the moon
pebbles light against her window
like a drunk admirer.

My daughter is coming
to the gravity of a body not wholly
her own anymore.

She is drowning in it, lungs
catching light like water,
panic weaving an orbit around her.

For the first time in her life
she can't see herself
as anything but reflected light,

as anything but alone.

ii.

When we were trying to conceive
I read endless fairy tales
about childless women

who were instructed to catch
two fertile fish and eat them
by the river, dripping with moonlight,

their bellies distended with food;
bodies aching fullness and emptiness.

iii

When boys come to puberty,
it is their desire that defines them,
stains the sheets
that their mothers wash and hang to dry.

Imagine being defined by what *you* desire.

iv.

It's like watching an eclipse,
this sudden erasure
of everything she knew

of the sky. People used to
bang drums and pots,
try and frighten off

the dragon swallowing
the sun. Now, we hold
hands and watch

the moon's shadow
through pinhole cameras.
A sun the size

of a newborn's fingernail.

v.

Maybe our bodies are
more honest.

Pain, deep within
the recesses of her body,
an ache she can't point to;

blood without
a wound.

vi.

Today #MeToo is trending.
Every women testifies
to their harassments

and assaults. I remember
so keenly being 12,
standing naked

in front of the mirror.
Thinking no one will
desire me, this body

will be hated and reviled.
I was wrong,
and right.

vii.

I am teaching her to fight.
This, I tell her, is how to drive
the soft bone of a man's nose

into his brain. This is how
to push an attacker off
from a mount position,

this is how to thread
your keys between
your knuckles when you walk.

This is how, when confronted
with a blade or gun,
you leave your body.

viii.

In fairy tales, women supplicants
find their children disguised as animals,
or once, even a round ripe melon.

The mother is sanguine about a fat gourd
for a daughter. Sends her rolling past
lions, demons, and men.

The melon goes to school,
teases her mother, tumbles about the town.
This child all bursting sweetness,

every road unspooling before her.

ix.

My daughter is afraid to break
down in public. In class,
after a test.

Anxiety curls onto her chest
like a cat suckling her sweater,
kneading her sadness.

Aretaeus named the womb
an animal within an animal;
a kind of wandering sorrow.

She knows now
that people are looking.
She learns to fake a smile.

x.

October, and on our walk home
the harvest moon is gold
against the velvet sky.

She talks and her words
spin like a revolver
in the fingers of an old west gun-slinger.

When did she learn to bridle
the night, to call in the sunset
for her ride?

xi.

In the story, no one breaks
the melon open. The daughter
simply unfolds herself

from the rind. A miracle,
all she has escaped,
how unbruised

her body. Even in stories
we can only imagine freedom
tucked inside a hard shell,

as having escaped, unbroken.

xii.

The moon edges closer,
nudging her arm but looking away.
A cat at the door,

it wants in and out,
howling at the existence
of the closed screen.

Your daughter sleeps,
her bones and dreams stretch
like the horizon.

All I can do is stay here,
prop open this creaky door,
letting her leave and come

back to herself,
and to me.

Globe

I am nothing but the empty net which has gone on ahead
of human eyes, dead in those darknesses,
of fingers accustomed to the triangle, longitudes
on the timid globe of an orange.
    — Pablo Neruda

All my ignorance is unspooling,
vast as the underwater light
of a pulsing squid. Dreams are stacked mirrors,
reflecting plates. My son wakes up and screams
that a monster has eaten his feet.
Who's to say he's wrong? In his bed
both his feet and his phantom feet, the monster
and me. I bring him water and tell him it was once a cloud,
one day his tears will salt the ocean bed.
I am nothing but the empty net which has gone on ahead.

My hands drip every time I bring them
to my eyes. God shakes the sea
and it's pretty as a snow globe, plastic flakes
shimmering in the slow, thick water.
My son abandons his bed and crawls into mine,
wonders why dreams hide in the crevices
of our minds. I tell him that we all have souls
like oysters, an unbearable brightness
beneath the cragged surfaces
of human eyes, dead in those darknesses,

in those skulls that carry a single lantern,
a false hope. Better to be blind
here, to grope for each other's hands in the dark,
to feel the ghosts as they shudder past, brushing
a foot, lifting a lock of hair from our cheeks.
What infinites. What magnitudes
are the reach of your questions
between our interlaced hands.
Read the equator of our lifelines, the latitudes
of fingers accustomed to the triangle, longitudes

of our limited reach.
I can hardly navigate this night,
the stars behind the clouds that were
once ocean, that lived inside all our ancestors
and enemies. Let it gather, open the windows
to the breath and tears and torrent
of the living wind, the phantoms, the monsters
who swim with us, in this suspended water
perched, turbulent and roaring,
on the timid globe of an orange.

Math for girls

Let's go exploring my daughter says,
and I remember how when she was 6
we would go into the backyard
with a butter knife, a flashlight,

and some cookies: intrepid explorers,
and so she steps onto the trail as I
do the math all women do, that she hasn't,
at 13, learned yet. Solving
for zero, calculating the odds

against the needle packets we've found there,
the isolation of the trail, the men
I've seen walking out of woods,
the whispered stories, the hairs

raised on the back of my neck. She's pulling
apart the curtain of weeds, calling out
to me as I consider my self-defense courses
and how traumatized she'd be if I told her

to run (and if she'd run) and how long
I could hold off 1, and if I could hold off 2
and how my phone is in my pocket
and if you can get to it you need to click

the power button rapidly to trigger 9-1-1
and are my location services on?
Let me go first, I say, and tuck
your pants into your socks to avoid ticks.

In the underbrush there is a cart
tipped to its side, ribs burnt,
a make-shift barbecue. It is beautiful
here, the heron stalking its way

through brackish water, the smell of fish
and leaves and extinguished fire.
Then a quick pull, a footfall
coming towards us; a young deer,

now frozen as we walk slowly on earth
that is charred and cold, black branches
crumbling underfoot, the faun
taut with the vigilance of prey.

The dreams of people who call 911 to complain after an Amber Alert

Every dreamer has a Midas touch, their cheeks glowing, their hands clawing at their chests, trying to dig out a trapped vein. Their dreams are urgent calls to their own children, frantic phones that ring and ring. Their dreams are balloons of blood, stretched thin as a membrane, suspended above their beds. Their dreams are choked canaries in mines of their skulls, those last few notes strangling a song they strain to hear. Their dreams are of their fathers, fish-mouthed, gasping for air. Their dreams are a silty river carrying everything past: a nub of bone, an ivory button, a doll whose face is an echo. Their dreams are a frightened girl, the fullness of her dark eyes, and god's forgiveness when they look away.

Dick pics

Two dicks, sitting in
my daughter's inbox,
like men without hats,
waiting for any door
to open.

*

Sighting a stranger's penis
used to be rare. Remember raincoats?
Like a flash of lightning,
like a Scratch 'N Win ticket—
sometimes glittering knock-off watches,
sometimes a flapping penis
shivering in the electric air.

*

Overcooked hotdog?
Aborted fetus?
Close up of a thumb?
Rolled baloney on a lonely deli plate?

*

We have whole monologues
for vaginas. But I can only imagine
a penis as silent,
which isn't the same
as listening.

*

The lighting is never
good. No one ever drapes
a dick in folds of linen

with the head looking
back, one pearl earring
shining in stilled patience.

*

In the schoolyard
a graffitied cock stands on balls
pointing to the night sky—
a fallen constellation.

*

Women are for portraits,
lounging nudes stuffed into frames,
luminous and arch. They are heads
breasts, ass, and feet (though
never speech). You must pay
and cross a velvet rope to see them.

The penis stands alone
in filthy bars and bathrooms,
in wooded parks,
in the shadowed alleys
whistling a moon-white tune.

*

Now penises are everywhere.
Like posters for a one-act play,
plastered on every telephone pole,
bench, building, on every mailbox,
on your kitchen chair,

so that you have to push through piles of them,
great snowdrifts of dick.
Just to reach across the room
and tuck a stray hair
back into your daughter's braid.

The Far Right Marches on Charlottesville, 2017

Surely these boys were
beautiful, once. Their hands gentle
with a fallen bird, or over the ears
of a sister so she wouldn't hear
their mother beg for mercy,

these boys, who hold their fear
as tiki torches, who laugh
together; it looks so open
and so easy the way they lean
on each other tonight.

Is it motherhood or fear,
denial or hope,
that makes me want to believe
they don't understand what they want
when they sing their desire
to murder my children?

Wellness Check

We're just here for a chat.

Talk with your hands up. Talk with the bodies of your brethren rotting in your mouth. Talk to the black hole of my standard issue. Talk with your mouth full of carpet.

Everyone loves a man in uniform.

Here, my uniform marches in ahead of me, full of Kevlar confidence. My shirt is made of a hundred count stop and frisk cotton. My wife cleans it with OxiClean because nothing gets whites whiter.

I'm just standing here, trying to help, trying to do my job.

If I say I see the same monsters you do who gets to aim my taser?

I'm not dragging you, I'm escorting you to the car.

Remember how your mother used to slide her hand over the night-gloss of your hair before bed? Why is your hair so limp in my fist? I'll smooth it with my boot.

I get a thousand calls a day,

every door holds a monster, every window is broken. Every dark corner is an unending maze. Target practice is a black silhouette.

Can we come in?

Is this your house? Is this your car? Is this your skin? Is this your heart beating like a hummingbird's wings? Is this a picture of your father? Is this your blood?

I'm here to help.

You need to calm down. I took a week long course in de-escalation. The coffee was stale and the air-conditioning rattled like my mother's lungs before she died. Look, I'm making eye contact. I'm listening to whatever it is you're saying. I'm not actually touching my holster; I'm just hovering above it. I'm smiling.

Ma'am, we need you to calm down.

Your daughter learned to fly, that's all.

Cutting

The willow's branches sweep
the frozen pond, fingertips encased
in bells of ice, a skittering my dogs
can't resist and so they crash

through the thin surface,
lunging again and again
at the broken ice, even as their
paws turn a swollen red.

*

Years ago I flipped through your sketchbook.

God!

The precision, hours upon hours of casting
shadows with your pencil. And in the margins,
words small enough to be carved
into a grain of rice:
                              loser, slut

*

I haul the dogs out of the pond, tripping
and cursing, and think of you
falling through your skin,
the shock of blood, everything suddenly coursing and alive:
almost-spring under a wintered body.

*

It's almost always girls who cut:
pretty, academically inclined, perfectionists.
Girls who are good at being girls.

*

When you would come visit
you'd disappear upstairs and we'd hear
the heavy bag; that hard *thuuunk* sound
like a body hitting the ground,
giving in.

You never wore gloves and now I see
that was the point: you weren't hitting
the bag. You were being hit,
knuckles blistering and bleeding,
the perfect shade of red.

*

A boxing teacher once told me
that it's easy to teach women
how to throw a hard right,
but near impossible to get them
to make a sound.

*

It's not unhappiness. It's not a lack
of happiness. It's not a hole,
a black star or an emptiness.

*

On a road trip we played horrible
hypotheticals. *If you absolutely had to,*
who would you kill?

My daughter and I grabbed at answers
as if they were a cloud of mayflies surrounding us:
dictators, rapists, bullies, ex-boyfriends, film directors,
politicians, internet trolls

and your voice in the back
myself

you were the worst thing you could imagine.

*

Your favourite game was Cinderella. Remember?

I would hurl invectives at you while you
were on your knees, weeping quietly,
rubbing a coarse brush over the kitchen floor.

This is how we played.

*

When men get angry they punch walls,
or other men, or women.

*

Last year I sent you a famous poem:

You do not have to be good
You do not have to walk on your knees
For a hundred miles through the desert repenting.

I meant the lines to be prayers.
I thought of each word as a lit candle.
I thought the poem was a confessional.

Catching flight

Before we were married, we had
a small apartment, carpet worn
to paper, beige walls

like faces we might one day
try on. That first night I heard
a moth, dinner plate wings
serving wind.

In my sleep I thought
a dry ocean, waves of air
so hushed, dust falling

but of course, they were bats
and their small faces quaked
with fear, wide-eyed in the sky
of our ceiling.

We learned to catch them
by floating a windbreaker
over their suspended flight.

Weight enough to net
their wings, pin them to the carpet.
Every night I'd release
a few back outside

like black flowers
blossoming from the chest
of my coat.

She just wants attention

February wears last night's dress
on a walk of shame. Some guys holler
from dorm windows but most of us
pull the blankets up tighter,

not wanting to see the bare
branches or the birds
that pick at sore berried lips.

February, you have footprints
all over you—smudged mascara,
tulle of sodden red construction paper
trailing weakly from the recycling.

Go to bed and we won't ask you
who crushed the sky into a blotchy grey,
or if that whip-crack whimpering

of the lake is you, splintering
beneath the surface.

How to fill the void inside you

Buy yourself some flowers. Remember how your son would snap the necks and petals would break apart in his chubby fist? Everything should die so beautifully.

*

Relax in a beige room replete with orchids and music that includes small, soothing bells. Notice that your heel is dissolving into dead skin, your body is a cloud full of snow. All you have to do is watch it fall.

*

Make sure you drink enough water to flush out every cell. Make your body a river, always flowing away from the source. Be cold enough and fast enough to bleach the bones of the animals that drown within you.

*

Walk until you wear out three iron shoes, three iron hats, and fill three iron pitchers with your tears. Let a falcon drink from your pitchers, make a nest of your worn and crumpled hats. The chicks born from your misery will always find their way back to you.

My Boy

My young son begs for a toy gun. I
keep telling him, "it isn't okay
to pretend to hurt someone"

and restrain his fists from hitting.
And yet, I've taken up Krav Maga
and Kickboxing. I dream of them,

combinations twisting the sheets,
euphoria of knuckles biting into a face.
Every day, I pack my son off to daycare,

to careful cots and whole grain
snacks before sneaking off to class,
kicking until my shin bruises.

I practice delivering elbows
to the soft joint of skull and neck,
I choke out my opponents.

I don't know why I need this.

*

Today rain walks
in clouds over the fields,
mist touching each bent stalk

with spring benedictions
of remembering.
This is how we walk

in our minds,
our gaze a light rain,
a mist of what's gone.

Yesterday I read of men
who were given a choice:

15 minutes to sit with their thoughts,
or an electric shock.

Most chose the current,
the body lightning,
wildfire to raze the field —

pain: a brilliant forgetting.
When will this come
to my boy?

When will he be so scared
to walk in his own field
that he sets it alight?

*

Superheroes infect the house.
They're like stink bugs,
thousands hiding in every
corner, bodies rattling

their invincibility. With my daughter it was
princesses, slippery silks veiling
everything pink. It was easier
to shear through

the princess appeal. Do you *want*
to be locked in a tower? To scrub
floors? To dance on knives,
eternally silent?

How do you argue against
winning every fight? Flexing
a grin and never having l'esprit
d'escalier? Sprinting to save

everyone, all the time? Look at
Superman. His x-ray vision cuts into his dreams:
bodies exploding like planets,
and him, alone in the darkness

of infinite space.

*

Mommy, I love you for
ever and ever and I won't
ever hurt you

he says in his jammies,
hand reaching through
the slats in his crib

to stroke my arm.
It's been a day of rages,
of kicks and bites:

my wrist wears a bracelet
of teeth marks
like tiny raised pearls.

Just before bed, exhausted,
he leans on a magazine rack
and the thin wood collapses

in his hand. He bends
forward, tips his head
to the floor like a kneeling

ancestor before the gods,
and weeps
for all he's broken.

*

Before dinner, he hides behind
his chair; tells me he is alone
and it is raining
and he has no family
and he is oh-so-hungry

won't I let him in?

#MeToo

"Language is the house with lamplight in its windows / visible across the fields...."
    — Anne Michaels

Language is the house with lamplight in its windows
but the body is a grassy field
filled to the brim with starlight.

Slip among the dark blades —
you are that creature
who is both prey

and predator. Lamplight is
a caged fury. Wouldn't this house
look brilliant on fire,

an imploding
star,

reaching out?

Seven dreams about my son

i.

Isaac was Sarah's only son, and here he sits, on a stone of sacrifice. The stone is wide as the earth, flat as the sky.

ii.

When he was coiled inside me, I knew nothing of him. Unnamed, all I knew was his sex. Every day the news christened another murdered woman. Another lit lantern on that windless sea. I wondered if they passed, loosened souls becoming and unbecoming.

iii.

My body slept through his delivery. Sliced open, I felt only the tugging of the doctor as they pulled him into the lights. My back arched to follow him, then collapsed; I was tied to the table.

iv.

Isaac, full of laughter. Sarah was barren, too old for children. Isaac came to her like a lily blooming in brackish waters. Pure, whole. Dazzling.

v.

I have raised a girl—I know how to braid hair and slip fear into her pocket like a stone. She carries it with her always, rubbing the surface until her body knows the shape. What do I give you Isaac?

vi.

You were laughing in your sleep, toothless mirth. Head thrown back, silk hair curling into the sweat of your scalp. I have an animal love for you. I want to carry you in my mouth, hide you in a burrow of earth; you make me feral.

vii.

What do I give you? Put down your burden of wood and rope. Don't hold another's faith. Open your hands. Walk off the edge of the earth.

Spawning Grounds

Your teeth are made of fish
my son says, and my mouth
spawns, swimming in
the shallows of language.

Every night I dream of teeth:
we hold a paper bag
and scatter molars to paddling ducks,

or my teeth are melting stalactites
and I offer him handfuls
of thick, silted water.

My son, every time I try to open
my mouth to you I am a gasping,
hooked creature

and my words swim, dark and wet

against your bared skin,
prehensile language
grasping to hold you.

His True Self

The writer, on a stage, told us his children couldn't be happy
unless he wrote, thereby exposing them to his true self.
The women in the room
quietly passed around the side-eye
like a platter of cucumber sandwiches.

What an asshole, you might think,
But his true self paints eyes on
the blind and floats like an angel
above the dishes
and the too-tight shoes and the half can of
baked beans growing mold in the refrigerator
and the top that exposes the beginnings of breasts
in your twelve year old and you don't want to slut-
shame her and she's comfortable in it and the school
will call you about it later, you know. His true self

wakes at 6:30 every morning for his writing
practice, because it takes discipline to step over
the dog shit in the hallway and past the toy truck lying
prone on the stairs, and to not look
at the calendar which is rapidly running,
sprinting really, towards the end of the month and there's
maybe not enough money for swim lessons unless the city
subsidy comes through, but that's for kids in grade nine and she's
only in grade eight this year, isn't she? His true self,

who is not an asshole, thinks deeply about Derrida
and the ethics of reading, and his true self
writes poems that are so beautiful
he feeds them to his children,
and they open their mouths like birds
and their bones shine through their skin
so luminous and whole is their happiness.

How to leave your child at daycare for the first time

Don't prolong it. Say goodbye firmly. Cleave
the air between the two of you with a machete.
Let him know his bones will have to hold him.
Point to the clock, show him how the hands
tremble like a stunned bird after hitting a window.
Let him take something from home, a shard
of glass maybe, or your beating heart.
Start a goodbye routine; have him watch
as you walk away, shedding a thousand
hollow corpses of who you were;
a trail of chokecherries for him to follow home.

Rescue

for S & S

Bring me your pain, love. Spread
it out like fine rugs, silk sashes,
warm eggs, cinnamon
and cloves in burlap sacks. Show me
— Ellen Bass

My friends and I are all in the middle of a crisis.
A daughter who cannot bear life, a husband
whose departure cracks the marrow of the house;
my own daughter lost and wandering in the forest
of her body. All of us, staring at our empty
teacups realizing we read
our leaves wrong. Here we are, re-training as first-responders,
digging through the rubble. Even recovery dogs are given
volunteers who pose as rescuable, among the dead.
Bring me your pain, love. Spread

your map of the disaster area and we'll pretend
to rescue each other. We'll wind ropes around one another
to descend into that windless place.
Who knew that parenting would be so much searching
blindfolded, calling *Ollie Ollie Oxenfree*, our shaky voices
giving us away. Now, sifting through the ashes
of their early childhoods, its intense quick burn,
we look for the raw singed bird who is supposed to rise,
but instead gasps the air and thrashes
fire out like fine rugs, silk sashes,

breath beaten as dust rises in the wind.
This is the secret of being a woman, we tell them.
The fire that consumes you is ashes in the mouth,
and though no one else does, we will always believe you
when you say you burn. I know it seems
like a thin balm, but let us bring it to you anyway,
folded in the aprons of our skirts,
the way we used to carry windfall apples.
Let us listen, stroke your hair, and cook up infinite
warm eggs, cinnamon

spiced cookies, milky chai. Don't dismiss
the sanctity of casseroles. Of midnight phone calls
and the women who offer to take a bat
to your ex's car. May our girls discover that rescues
happen as you link hands in the underbrush
and call out into the night. That what you see
in the face of your friend's despair is your own
soul. And so you learn to hold her face, and yourself, gently.
You unwrap each other and find beauty. Like myrrh, figs, tea,
and cloves in burlap sacks. Show me

Portrait of a marriage

Upstairs, the baby curls between us
like a comma,
a pause or a breath.

This morning the clouds are too tired
to float. They've landed here to lick
their wounds, faces

up against the kitchen window
like a hangover. Why is nothing put
away? Even the night

hangs in the edges of the doorway,
reluctant to put on its coat.
I am in every room of this house

sweeping yesterday
into the bin.
Putting away the toys—

wide-eyed babies, a hammer,
a sauce pan holding a bun and a tiny
bulldozer. Leftovers of a pretend life.

I just want to be a good day

I just want to be a good day.
To button the clouds on tight
and pull the sunrise out with a flourish
like a handkerchief.

I want to walk by the internet
without snagging on the comments,
without being pulled to pieces
by a long fraying thread.

I want to line up the hours
like glass bottles at the fair
and shoot them one by one—
plink, plink, plink, plink

until the counter is an emptied horizon.

Come in the speaking silence of a dream

My father comes in dreams,
an arm slung around a park
bench, casual as the dove
cooing at my feet.

Every single time I waste
his presence. I argue his death
even as I look
through my pockets

for my children
or half-remembered prints.
I wish I could dream
better, instead of plodding

through as I insist that, no,
he *is* dead
even as he is here,
even as he is the mourning

dove, even as he is sugar
becoming a ghost on my tongue.

Cottage Visits

At our friend's cottage all the kids run
to the shore with their Barbie and Diego fishing rods:
summer after summer they stand at the dock
and pull up tiny sunfish and pickerel,
fish so eager they leap from the water for bait.
The first time our son is old enough to join in,
he half believes that a fish will come up begging for life,
sloughing wishes like scales on the wet dock.

I hate this part of the visit. I stand at the edge
of the of the lake, shivering, dreading the minute
a child pulls up a convulsing creature,
puckered mouth opening and closing like a heart's valve.
Once a pickerel wrapped itself, serpentine,
around my arm, its muscles pulsing, its grip
as desperate as a woman trying to claw away
hands from her throat. When we came to the cottage

in the winter, we walked on water, fish tucked
into beds of mud beneath our feet. We thundered
above them in a toboggan, shaking the foundations
of their sky with our boots. But now we reach
into their world and our children will hold them,
our host will pick up a small hammer and cave
in the soft bones of their heads.
After the first catch, my son watches in awe

as the walleye is handed to me and I cut the head, cleanly,
scissor open the belly. I pull on the flesh and the gnathic
bones open with a crack. The gorge contains a minnow,
whole somehow, and my son, looking over my shoulder
mistakes it for a baby, it is so small, and perfect,
and still. He takes it, carefully, and lays it in the water,
with the tenderness of a wish.

Worms

This spring is heavy with floods,
earth nodding a hundred blind
and sodden heads. How pink and unguarded,
how exposed. They remind me of men

and as I'm thinking this, my young son
screams and sidesteps the slow, wet flesh
beneath him. *They're just worms*, I tell
him, but he trembles and says *snakes*

with the authority of Adam
blessing each animal with its true nature.
Worms, butterflies, chickens:
my son's fears grow every day.

They grow so amorphous
that even my voice from another room
is a snake loose in the house.
He tells me that he is not afraid of tigers,

polar bears, or dinosaurs. That he could
beat up a ninja. That if a bad guy
came in the house
he would cut his head off

with a butter knife. At night, in bed, I rub
his chest, feel the outlines of his ribs
that curve together like the hold
of a ship. What is contained

in this boat? All his fears, two-by-two,
feral in the rocking sea of his blood.
I want to tell him the end of the story:
a dove, new arable land

even as the ocean rises around us.

Dispatches

He brings home snowmen,
q-tipped arms waving
like a flag on the horizon:
evidence of another country.

Kindergarten is a foreign language,
dispatches come in pieces—
a horse came to school today—
and I don't know if it was a puppet,

a police horse, or a well-decorated
cake. Sometimes he is so exhausted
after school that he melts
into a snowsuited puddle

on the doorstep, unable to lift a mitten
or speak. I kneel by his side
and peel off his foxy hat and his mitts,
pull off his boots one by one,

unzip his coat, his snow pants, his sweater,
my hands sweeping his flushed skin
like an archeologist's brush, trying to read
the small marks the day has left on him.

Make lemonade

Open your mouth.
Let me pluck your loosened
teeth, a palm full of porous
white clouds.

Give me your hair,
not the lock, but the root,
the part that knows
how to hold.

Why are you crying?

Part your ribs
like the sea,
like dry ground in the mist,
like a virgin, bleeding.

Seat 8b

On the train, the first cold snap of December.
The wind ripples over the lake
like a man rolling a coin

between his knuckles.
For a minute I feel such vertigo
it seems as though we are flying:

what is ice, or cloud, or steam,
or sky? Remember making clouds
of our breath? Popeye cigarettes

chalky between our clenched teeth
as we stomped the schoolyard
in our moon-heavy boots.

Remember the altered gravity of play
that had us bounding between
bells into worlds with as many

suns as we could conjure
between us? The stranger beside
me looks up at the same time,

his face caught in the reflected
clouds, and I imagine we are
both thinking of the drifting

stratus of our bodies;
the clouds that once sailed
inside us.

First Contact

Workers in large white suits,
helmets like astronauts,
float around the sidewalk
filling vials and plastic baggies.

They work slowly, yellow
tape defining territory,
newly claimed by a body.

I walk here every day
the dog picks up the scent
of a man's last breath.
How do we live

in this new atmosphere?
Hard-looking men from
the street clinic bare

their teeth in helpless smiles,
do everything but
put their hands up in a gesture
of surrender,

peace, or an attempt
to make first contact
across the void.

In order to become men

with the same tight mouth,
and the young man and my son and I
all born helpless in order to become men
the way birds are born naked
  — Richard Harrison

My son brandishes a sword at me
and we pretend to cut each other down,
bloodless. He has already mastered the art
of a stoic face as I lop off his arm
now you say 'I win!' and, if you want you can say it
in girl language. As if gender were geography, north and south,
and we didn't all speak the same clean
tongue of violence.
My son, we are the same throughout,
with the same tight mouth,

the same clenched heart, a fist
holding its only coin.
My combatives class is filled with men;
paratroopers, prison guards, and cops
who have to secure their handguns before class.
I'm the only poet, but I get the same high.
Once, after I was knocked down, the young instructor
slung his arm round my neck, ground his knuckle into my hair;
we were sweat-slick and laughing and bleeding, and it was
    enough that I had tried
and the young man, and my son, and I

65

knew in our bones that violence is a kind of fire
that can solder men together
or temper in the body like a blade.
What is it to raise a boy? I do want him to feel
that power, to be knocked down and raised up
again by his brothers, to limp away, having spent
every cell of his blood's rush.
My son, the poetry of it is the moment on your back,
the knowledge of us once again
all born helpless in order to become men,

and it is a miracle to become at all.
Did I ever tell you about your father?
How when he was nineteen, walking me home,
both of us drunk, he brought me to his house
and took my hands while I cried about *my* father
who was dying? He held my grief like it was sacred
and I saw then what kind of a man he would be,
tenderness shot through his bones like marrow,
like flight in a hatchling awakened;
the way birds are born naked.

Notes

The glosa "Angstrom" begins with an epigraph from "Postludium" by Tomas Tranströmer as it appeared in his *Selected Poems, 1954-1986*, edited by Robert Hass.

The glosa "Globe" begins with an epigraph from "Enigmas" by Pablo Neruda.

The glosa "Rescue" begins with an epigraph from "Basket of Figs" by Ellen Bass from her book *Mules of Love*.

The glosa "In order to become men" begins with an epigraph from "The Creative Writing Teacher Writes to His Wife" by Richard Harrison from his book *On Not Losing My Father's Ashes in the Flood*.

The epigraph in "#MeToo" is from Anne Michaels's poem "What The Light Teaches" from her book *Poems*.

The lines quoted at the end of "Cutting" are from Mary Oliver's poem "Wild Geese" from her book *Dream Work*.

The poem "Come in the speaking silence of dream" takes its title from the Christina Rossetti poem "Echo".

Acknowledgements

Excerpts from this book, sometimes in different versions, have appeared in *Grain Magazine, The New Quarterly, Prairie Fire, Vallum, The Malahat Review, The Moth* (UK) and *CBC books.* Thank you to the editors.

Thanks to the Canada Council for the Arts and the Ontario Arts Council as well as the juries who believed in this book project.

Thank you to Richard Harrison for your care and attention with these poems as well as your generosity. Thanks to Jim Johnstone whose incisive edits were always, maddingly, absolutely correct.

Thanks to Poetry In Voice for supporting the work of Canadian poets and for creating the next generation of poets and readers. Thanks to YGK Combatives for letting me punch my feelings out and also for being such a solid group of guys who happen to enjoy total domination in street fights.

Thank you to those who sustain, inspire, and awe me: Sadiqa, Susan, Ashley, Kirsteen, Ying, and Nancy Jo. I couldn't ask for a better coven/writing group. Thanks to the BDL, who always know when I need a beer. To Matt, Kendra, John, Harriet, Megan and Andrew — thanks for making me eat too much, drink too much, and stay out much too late. You've probably been a detriment to the writing but a mainstay to my sanity.

Thank you to mom, my most consistent and ardent fan. Thank you to Abby, who knows that hardly anyone reads poetry and so allows me to write about her. Thank you to Isaac, who hopefully won't be mad about me writing about him. And to Theo, for being the bright little light who was born the day after I submitted this manuscript. For Tim, thanks for being funny and sweet and knowing when I need a second main course. xo

Sarah Yi-Mei Tsiang is the author of the poetry books *Status Update* (2013), which was nominated for the Pat Lowther Award, and *Sweet Devilry* (2011), which won the Gerald Lampert award. Her work has been longlisted (2018) and shortlisted (2019) for the CBC Poetry Prize and the UK's Forward Prize for Best Single Poem. Her work has appeared in *Best Canadian Poetry* (2013, 2020) and *Best of the Best Canadian Poetry* (2017). She is the editor of the poetry anthology *Desperately Seeking Susans* (2013), the Creative Director for Poetry In Voice, and the Poetry Editor for *Arc Poetry Magazine*. She is also the author of several children's books.